The Phoenix Living Poets

STILLS

Poets Published in
The Phoenix Living Poets Series

★

JAMES AITCHISON

ALEXANDER BAIRD · ALAN BOLD

R. H. BOWDEN · FREDERICK BROADIE

GEORGE MACKAY BROWN

HAYDEN CARRUTH · JOHN COTTON

JENNIFER COUROUCLI

GLORIA EVANS DAVIES

PATRIC DICKINSON

TOM EARLEY · D. J. ENRIGHT

JOHN FULLER · DAVID GILL

PETER GRUFFYDD

J. C. HALL · MOLLY HOLDEN

JOHN HORDER · P. J. KAVANAGH

RICHARD KELL · LAURIE LEE

LAURENCE LERNER

CHRISTOPHER LEVENSON

EDWARD LOWBURY · NORMAN MACCAIG

JAMES MERRILL · RUTH MILLER

LESLIE NORRIS · ROBERT PACK

ARNOLD RATTENBURY

ADRIENNE RICH · JON SILKIN

JON STALLWORTHY

GILLIAN STONEHAM

EDWARD STOREY · TERENCE TILLER

SYDNEY TREMAYNE

LOTTE ZURNDORFER

STILLS

by

CHRISTOPHER
LEVENSON

CHATTO AND WINDUS

THE HOGARTH PRESS

1972

Published by
Chatto and Windus Ltd
with The Hogarth Press Ltd
42 William IV Street
London W.C.2

★

Clarke, Irwin & Co. Ltd
Toronto

ISBN 0 7011 1832 6

Distributed in the United States of America
by Wesleyan University Press

ISBN 0 8195 7041 9

Printed in Great Britain by
Lewis Reprints Ltd
London and Tonbridge

For Harro and Carina Bouman

ACKNOWLEDGEMENT

Some of the poems in this book have been published in the following journals and anthologies: Arlington Quarterly, Best Poems of 1969, CBC 'Anthology', Canadian Forum, Fiddlehead, Malahat Review, Micromegas, Poetry Review, Queens Quarterly, Seneca Review.

Contents

Travelling West

Unyielding, held at a distance,
the reticence
of rock strata, unbroken
silence
skylined with mountains.

Halfway there, the foothills,
filed down, are day-long-re-
defined by wheeling slants
of shadow as towards evening
cloud shafts light upon
abandoned farms that the grasses
have taken over.

Not statements, suggestions.
Mind too can found its meanings in
rock faces, stone walls, a quality
of stacked peat and smokedrift
over rivers broad as daylight.
Texture is enough.

Iowan Spring

Too quick,
in parenthesis. Already
summer encroaches
with warm odours of pine
before the bloated rivers
subside.

A flurried spate of green
unfurls overnight,
blurring every outline.
What I miss —
the slow awakening,
hamlets unfolding in the comely downs,
mists skeining the junctions
to lift into keen air
crisp with woodsmoke
a hesitant tenderness.

Salt Lake City

The cratered landscape replete
with lights, one came upon it
suddenly after the gorges
at three one night last spring,
the sky clear after snowstorms.
Nothing of course to see
in all the clean, wide streets
but dead stone; grass-blown runways
at the city's edge, a row of houses
like tank-cars abandoned in mid-prairie,
and the lights,
a mirage of hope between mountains.
From here the missionaries
radiate over salt flats, deserts,
race westwards to redeem
the promised land
so long in pawn,
Reno, Las Vegas.

El Paso

I stayed there one whole summer,
admiring at night the totem skyscrapers
and at dawn the sun picking out in gold
adobe walls on the Mexican side,
teeth in a broken skull.

They call it El Paso
because, it seems, long since,
that brown trickle, the Rio Grande,
would flood mile-wide each spring
and hamper the trek for gold:
here was a crossing-place.
The baroque cathedral
belongs now to Mexico,
where every harsh winter
hill indians die of cold,
squatting inside tin hovels
and thinking what they see
across the border, supermarkets,
tidy apartments for rent,
must somehow be meant for them too.

That's all I know of its history
because not much has been left showing:
buildings have covered it up or freeways
to the airport and the bookstore
ten miles out.

It is still the frontier.

Metropolis

The city is
heartless, all suburb,
parkways, driveways, spacious
residential areas. Ask
for the centre, they'll show you
two streets intersecting.
When the lights say go
people carry on walking
through heated arcades and into
subways, department stores,
up escalators. Watch this space. There is
no fountain in the square
to linger by, not even a pompous
equestrian statue, there is
no square, where in 1900
a warehouse stood and a bar
and an open space waiting for something
to happen in it or with it.
It happened: its sheer glass sides
twenty-six storeys high
reflect the confidence of
the million shareholders of
Mutual Insurance. Its penthouse
restaurant is the best place
from which to view the whole city —
parkways, driveways, spacious
residential areas.

Nevada

After so much mere salt, rock, desert
                              "somehow we must restore
                              a balance to nature"
quickie divorces, conveyor-belt marriages,
an incessant ringing of bells,
four lemons, three plums and a peach,
the perfect combination!
                              in every saloon
automats ply the automats with dimes.

Foiled by so much desert,
cut glass makes as good a show
as diamond. From a passing car
beer bottles look the same.

Every afternoon, starting at the Casino,
a tour of the testing grounds:
                    "after so long a peace
                    this country needs a war
                    to restore our moral fibre, to preserve
                    all that we hold dearest."
This time, maybe, the jackpot.

In Reno, Las Vegas, reserves
for millionaires, a conservationist
proposes a wild-life sanctuary
for the last of the great predators.
With sprinklers working the lawns ten hours a day,
civilisation 'a soil for the most living'
is still a precarious foothold. Winds
will erode it, or we lose our nerve.

Ecology: checks and balances.
In Utah, the next state,
a silent majority, of sheep,

14

6000, dying, relinquish
their place in the sun
that incarcerates our waste.
                    "At the brink of disaster
                        America must not be caught off balance"

In this promised land there is no shade, only
the acrid smoke of tires and money burning.
No speed limits, so why
stop? Hurry on. Hurry back.

Epitaph For A Killer

where so much had gone wrong
from the start, maybe
it was too late for surgery and only
a cop's bullet could cut away
the malignant tumor, life.

'senseless' they said as dozens
sprawled dead or wounded on Austin's
sidewalks, the elect, picked out, cut down
through telescopic lenses as he squatted
in his eyrie at the top
of the university's bookstore,
the uncut movie of his life
narrowed and focussed on a single frame.

'shocking' the neighbours said,
looking up from weeding
their neat lawns into TV cameras,
'that his single deed should earn
our neighbourhood of ordinary good people
such notoriety . . . where did we go wrong?
He had enough of everything.'
Shocking no-one had noticed
the stray footage accumulating,
violence already
a family tradition:
guns instead of pictures lined the walls
but never a word said
that was carefully weighed and loaded.

It was all 'you know what I mean'
and 'it's kinda hard to explain'
till all the inexplicables coalesced
in a single deficiency,
a sickle in the blood.

A Grammar Of Dissent

Their mood active,
the demonstrative adjectives — that filthy book,
this unwashed hippie, those unrepeatable slogans —
parade in front of the proper nouns — White House, Nixon,
        Dow —
and walk on the park's freshly-painted, keep-off grass.

But strong words, their mood imperative,
want 'to prevent trouble', decline
to hear parts of speech, direct address,
instead make a few examples —
tell those copulative infinitives to stop it at once! —
and question their antecedents.
Strong verbs, wanting to govern,
abbreviate the meeting, arrest
a weak verb with an irregular past.
The common nouns,
leaving their definite articles to litter the grass,
flee before run-on lines of auxiliaries
or are dragged off to begin a sentence.
Later the dependent clauses will return
to collect their principle parts.

Their mood passive,
the crowd of collective nouns
gathers to watch the fun. (The lovers,
observing concord, do not look up, recall
in parenthesis the simple past, try to forget
this continuous present.)
And we too, tomorrow, returning
will find only
the past perfect, the future conditional.

17

Notes For Foreign Students

An American is an animal that has
red blood, two arms, two legs,
one blind eye, one deaf ear,
and a heritage — automatic and fully loaded.

He's a delicate beast who lives on
newspaper pulp and celluloid
but spits out the cores.

His relationships are strictly 'personalized'
and disposable. He likes to be liked,
but also likes to move on.

If he asks 'How are you today?'
say 'fine' or 'real good',
bare your teeth in a wide grin.
It is impolite
to be unhappy in public.
Have fun!

The mint says, 'In God we trust',
the post office says, 'Pray for peace',
but to be on the safe side
Wall Street invests in rockets.

Money talks:
'One nation under God',
but only just.

Introduction To Cancer Diagnosis

Watch for these danger signs:
a sore that will not heal,
any unusual swelling, even of pride,
hoarseness, or difficulty
in swallowing all you are offered,
being always out of breath,
not lying easily
even at night, under darkness.
Remember, watch all your actions:
this disease attacks the whole system.

Arrested in time, we can save
if not your face, at least
your skin.

But if still in any doubt
about your condition,
wait till it bleeds.
Then you will know.

Then it is too late.

Freshman

Corn-fed Nebraska
bullocks, stubborn, bewildered
at the Field House they herd together
to register for classes. Later, in bars,
grasping ham-fisted at girl or beer,
always 'one of the boys'. They shy at ideas,
minds elsewhere, set
on horsepower, womanflesh, games —
proving themselves. At the Frat House,
in rut, on the football field,
wherever in unison they can shake off
the discomfort of not knowing,
they are magnificent.

Co-Ed

She smiles but she is plastic like the roses,
de-odorized, seedless; like roses
she will not crease or lose her shape
(gift-wrapped in skin-tight slacks and sweaters,
foam-rubber-padded where it matters most)
Age cannot wither her, she'll stay fresh
a year or two, then easily disposable,
knows how to arch an eyelid, whom to read,
and now, no tell-tale stains,
finds love like taking a shower
or mixing highballs, easy
after the first time.
Just gaze at her long enough, she'll respond, her plastic
smile flickers on like sky-signs, fades like roses.

Members Of The Faculty In Their Lounge

In their natural habitat
they are less unbending.
Some I have seen stoop
to pour coffee, hunch over chess boards.

Wall-to-wall sea-green carpets
under concealed lighting
insulate the bright armchairs
like tropical islands.

Each is autonomous.
Not all look like scholars.
This one, bestowing smiles, could be
a chubby business man,

while there a cleric intones
Chaucer or with a colleague exchanges
limp pleasantries; another
is in turn Hal, Falstaff, Lear.

The even light subdues them,
shadows scarcely impinge on
the carpet's moratorium, the primrose wall.
The professors relax into silence.

The Barnacle
for J.S.

Squat, crew-cut on his swivel-
chair, he seeks to
uphold the dignity
of office:

the bare desk's polished surface
reflects a mind hygienically
free of ideas.
Pencils, rulers, clips
are strategically deployed
to outflank the hard
questions, his forte
not strategy but
tactics, his bedside reading
timetables, agendas. Maybe
he cannot help being
'in the humanities',
but hates the word's
lush connotations.

Being set mainly on
staying put, crustacean,
this chairman under stress
clings to the rock of custom.

Bread And Marble Egg
for Gail and Mary Kubik

What is it in marble makes
its brooding silence, even fragmented,
stronger than common stone?
Less human? Perhaps. But these parapets,
statues, altars, pillars that no longer
uphold the invincible gods are still
too wholly man's — relics acquiring warmth
through centuries of human tenderness. I saw
an old priest absent-mindedly stroking the hair
of stone angels in the chapter-house.

One Easter we spared
ten days for the eternal city,
staying with friends explored
Rome layer upon layer, disinterring
from school-book memories
slain columns. In San Clemente
tenth-century frescoes and, below,
Mithraic vaults where the stone bull
still bellows for sacrificial
blood, the mask
outlives the face.

Admiringly in Gail's apartment we hold
two marble eggs, our hands
closed on their veined coolness,
one blue, one white. Have them, Mary said.
At lunch next day her brother-in-law,
good-humoured Boston minister, looked perplexed
like a Boxer dog that we found
so much in marble, sustenance, a gift
no more than itself, useless
for cooking, a thing. He took
a crust of bread from the wine-stained

wooden table, as if by saying
'bread', breaking a crust
in the shabby trattoria
he could create
a sacrament beyond art.

What we held to
was not idea but form:
behind these veins nothing
can grow, be shared, multiply,
no pounding heart, no simple
stone solutions, but coherence,
by right of inherited calm,
grain, texture, a shape
to make palm and fingers happy,
like trailing in water,
caressing abundant hair.

In fossils' deep-freeze antiquity
humblest artifacts yield
something of man, his touch,
simple love or fear, in trivia.
We scrape at coins, knives, pots
and finding, wonder
how they give eloquence
to civilizations struck dumb,
how they contain.

Throw loaves to the crusted beggar
who lurks enbalmed in sunlight
two thousand years:
there are still other ways
of starving.

Rather exact from stone
contours of swaying light,

gestures men die for, rescue
lost dignity, pride estranged,
and in this seeming
coldest art compound
in form the infinite possible
world, textures of living.

It is stone
restores what is most human.

The Quartet

After the velvet hush
the first chords assail us
gathered in darkness to watch
the intent, horn-rimmed, screwed up
concentration
of four foreign, middle-aged gentlemen
consorting *maestoso*,
bowing and scraping.

Out of the fidget
Brahms slowly emerges
like the Brocken, misty
and far off and under
another name.
Four spotlights, one over each
perfectly preserved specimen
(a 1750 viola, a violin
from 1672)
skewer these aural butterflies
to their sheets, only the frockcoats
and the black forelock of the one
who is not bald (but perspiring)
presume
to follow other rhythms.

By now the mind has wandered
so far from the auditorium
that it takes a whole avalanche
of flurried sound to return us
to darkness and the strings' predictable
twitter. The lento massage
of rich sound,
plangent agonies over-rehearsed into
monochrome, are barely in time to
dither once more into a final

reverie, and chase it with a frenzied
rush towards silence.

At last they are bowing, the four
earnest musicians, and leaving
allegro for refreshments, ma non troppo,
to our half-lit applause.

Watch The Birdie

In the pound my lobsters boiled; outside
at the cold sea's edge I watched
a herring gull's sharp bill
wrench at a crab, unpick
the neat purse, then tug out
liver and furry membranes.
His talons plucked
the still convulsive flesh
and had half gulped it down
before I turned away.

Then with a pocket knife
I unclamped a sea-urchin,
scrubbed off its spines
and gouged the living centre till its soft
innards spewed out like yolk,
rinsed the remaining yellow
pulp with sea water,
and left it to dry, a perfect
specimen. Mauve-green,
its segments, fretsaw-serrated,
when broken make brittle
traceries of shell, geometric
patterns in filigree, exact.

I turned back to my poem,
toyed with an idea,
an elegy for a broken home,
but could not construct
its intricate cadences
with always the gulls veering
and standing off as if in
expectation, their harsh cries
mocking, tu quoque, tu quoque.

The Lost City

Fall light through latticed windows; mist, lanterns merge
dissolving ulterior shades. Tacit among
decaying colonnades the lovers
have grown embalmed with moss, their echoed
cries mere whisper and groping fingers become
implicit with leaf. Lenient winds

scarcely once all night long stray through these squares
to drift with leaves the ancient coolness of fountains
or unwind through passages, stairways, to the belvedere
where I stand, tenebral, gazing down on a city
lost under smoke but luminous, to overhear
its many baffled night sounds, catch its drift

of hasty farewells, and sift through memory
a half-heard language I no longer know
in a remote country. These fragments are first draft
of an imagined homeland. Fugitive, I remain here,
        hazarding
all, having come so far, on the one view
and learn through flight my foreshadowed destination.

Slowly at dawn the crucial light distances,
reconstitutes in the clear air castle, spire, bridge,
clock tower of vaulting gothic, stone, stone, opaque
now that night's conjectured skylines, blurred precincts,
emerge on the further shore, old houses moored
distinct and inaccessible. One day I shall go there.

The Burglar

'If entrance is effected by a trick — as when thieves say they have come
to read the meter for example — it is constructive breaking.'
— from an article on Burglars by Thomas Power in *The Observer,* 10/3/1968

'Gas Company,' I said. 'I've come to read your meter.'
The woman in the dressing-gown drew back, then smiled,
      then turned and
motioned me in. 'It's under the stairs,' she said.
'I know,' I said. 'I've done it here before.
These houses are all the same.'

When she brought me a cup of tea I took her arm
and with my usual deftness twisted it back
and with my spare hand clamped a chloroform pad
that I always carry with me for emergencies
over her lips. (I don't steal kisses.) Then like
the good judge of women I am I bound her over
to keep the peace with plaster all over her chops
and placed her with aplomb upon the sofa.

Among the debris of keepsakes, mirrors, appliances
I found nothing I needed: her supply of hope
was down to the last tablet.
I ran my fingers through her dresses, ransacked
trunks full of dirty linen, even the ice-box. Nothing.
It seems some people live on very little
between times.
Then under the welcome mat some sort of key,
which opened a curious casket under the bed.
It was full of promissory notes and IOUs
and proceedings for a divorce. This was not
what I had imagined when I entered, the house looked rich.

When the dumb blonde came to I was busy cramming
her last silk illusions into my bag. I apologized
for the mess, but at least it was a chance
for spring-cleaning, wasn't it?
And how else do we survive except by constructive breaking?

Old Friend

Each Christmas, grown apart, we find ourselves 'looking
        forward'
to meeting again, to 'getting to know your family';
each summer despatch some hastily-written card
from mountain-top or sea,

the encounter postponed; our memories overlook
announcements of birth or marriage, turning instead
to the limbo of photo albums, hoping pressed flowers, a
        pocket book
can restore communion with the comfortably dead.

But at last when time and place are right, one Easter driving
three days, we find you in a staid, upright house, are
        impressed
by the changes you have made, the kids. You look well, no
        doubt thriving
on your part-time social work — lay readers, your
        Christianity laced

with mild irreverence, a solid tastefulness and good sense
in furniture and causes. You make us feel at home, say
grace, promise happy returns . . . Should we on some pretence
better have stayed away?

Returning from Cuttyhunk, mist blanks the narrow straits;
        horns, bells
harrow the afternoon as the swaying ferry boat
drifts, engine off, all ears straining across the swell
for a buoy to clang. Time for a card. Yes, we are still afloat,

but stalled, with no bearings here. Into the yellowing leaves
I must have read more than the lines could bear.
Soon I shall bundle them, consign our vanished lives
to trash-can or bonfire,
admitting without lament that what now cleaves us
is stronger than what we share.

Maps

Slowly they fill in,
as civilization or blood spreads.
The misty coastlines
clear into archipelagoes,
lighthouses, harbours displace
the dragons and zephyrs.
Now roads, now railways
tentacle over drained marshes,
redeemed land.

It is settled. The intrepid
explorers return home
with fewer marvels each time and smaller
words; museums
cherish for us our first instinctive
survivals against winter,
stockades succumb to weeds.
Bearing, dividing our blood,
the rivers lose control
over their diverse landscapes.
Deltas proliferate,
our names breed history.

Maps die intestate, bequeath
the imagination nothing.
Insatiable as night,
the mind must plot each acre.
The latest Ordnance Surveys
predict a five-year growth
of motorway,
with every hamlet and tarn
named, every bridle path
shown; somewhere we need
a wilderness.
Small consolation

to stand by the family
car at the mountain top
trying to recall
that first journey
by night and without maps.

The Conspirators

It's not the sleeping alone that bothers me,
it's the furniture.
When we're all at home not a chair would squeak out of turn
but just let the family leave for a week and the housemaid
    fall sick,
they gang up on me, sofa and wardrobe, even the cabinet
I rescued from a bonfire and repainted,
that vicious Mexican mirror in the hall
and the kitchen table, but especially
the over-stuffed easy chair, he's the ringleader.

It's mostly in the small hours they hatch their plots
when they think I am asleep: the squat occasional table
stands guard as they meditate
obstruction, tripping devices.
The antiques are the worst. Where they learnt it from
I dread to think. But apart from the clichéd phrases
such as 'refusing to be sat upon', and the toilet bowl's
    threatening
'to punish me where it hurts most',
I have no idea where they stand on such major issues
as redecoration. And if they stage a revolt,
what do they gain by it? another owner? a junk shop?

Meanwhile I lie in bed and wonder
where we went wrong. We spring-clean the drapes each year
and polish the sideboards and have the beds re-sprung.
Perhaps we were too soft with them? Anyway, darling,
please come over tonight if you can, I need your company.
But remember to stand back when I open the door:
the sofa is liable to pounce.

The Facts Of Life

Parents and teachers, do not wait
until your children are about to die
before you tell them the facts of life:
they have a right to know.
Life, after all, is nothing shameful or unclean.
We are all implicated.
With the right people it can be a great adventure.
Nevertheless

    7 per cent of them will grow up maimed or blind
  15 per cent will be chronically undernourished
  38 per cent will be illiterate
  97 per cent will be ready to fight for their country
  11 per cent will answer 'I do not know'.

(children erode our calm with questionings
we had long since put by)

    one in twenty will become a consenting adult
    one in seventeen will become hooked on drugs
    one in fifteen will finish his education
       in Her Majesty's prisons
    one in ten will contract VD before the age of twenty
    (if not checked in time, love can be fatal)
    one in three of all their marriages will end in divorce.
    When asked 'Are you satisfied with your life?'
    one in five will answer 'I do not know'.

(only the fittest survive — arms dealers, union leaders, party
    bosses,
those who adapt, the grey ones who pass as white,
who tattoo their machine guns with words like 'love' and
    'the People')

    the world population will double by the year 2000
    its food supply will increase by maybe a third,

its supply of garbage, dumped trucks, oil slicks, polluted
    air will far exceed the demand,
our children will choke on our surfeiting.
When asked if they approve of purer water,
a quarter will answer 'how much
    will this increase our taxes?'

What makes this a poem and not a statistics lecture?
I don't care about the figures.
I saw one small boy crying and his mother dead.
I saw one blackened village. That was enough. All life is one.
I build my elegy on a single death.
The prison of the future grows from a single cell.

A Bad Trip

From quite close by I have seen them like islands
half lost under haze. You shout and nothing happens, words
flutter hither and thither like bats in the air between us
then seek their hollows out. At times
it was like attending a birth: she lay there
out of hearing, long black hair thickly tangled;
her nerves, sea-anemones, drift to the surface, float.
The simple words she asks for glow within
like supernovas in a blank sky.
She does not answer, moans.
Millennia ago was it
I spoke to her, Snow White
grappling with brackish undergrowths of dream,
slow motion of a mind reeling, a hand
groping finger by finger round a door
and nothing you can do.
Pulse after pulse recedes, conduits of fear
infest our night.
The black batteries of the brain discharge
their acid, go flat. Through her I wander
the horror of time like a wind tunnel,
lightless prairies blown clean,
'this little room an everywhere'.
I know her as she suffers,
voyeur, I stare
at the walnut skull split, its two wrinkled lobes
exposed, bringing to light
bitter sediments of desire, flushing her with
good grief!
        Slowly she comes to
herself, is re-collected, discards
the skin of darkness, assuming
on the derelict sofa
a daylight poise and pose. I do not know her.

In Flight

for Frederic Will

'Everyone has the highest
credentials
in a foreign country:
that's why we travel,' hopefully
to remain perfect strangers
to the inhabitants,
to our remaining selves.

Pasts of Vienna, Rome, —
themes in a fugue
acquiring meaning in time,
in the end, but not
to be played over. Home
is the stop after next,
a two-day touch-down
somewhere we passed through before
by chance,
another alias.

Les Libertins

Through bottle-glass darkly they saw the world
kaleidoscoped, more glittering, brighter the more
    fragmented,
and all at sea under a new system of stars:
why could not the lurching journey be all, end all?

A wench, a hip-flask. . . a window on the sea
shows only random flashes, riding lights,
a mirage of rocky headlands
and, beckoning still, the wreckers' lamp, despair.

In wine truth, perhaps. Imprisoned in this cave
of flesh, what else is there to do but grope, explore
by our own lights, a murky tallow flame,
the texture of floor and ceiling before they shrink
forcing us inwards to the pit, before
we are rendered down, smearing our gold with fat.

Nude

Through eyes half shut, yes,
they might have seemed dunes,
those young breasts, or the groin
a mirage of trees.
It is a woman, nude.
Only the shadows drape her
cadence of arm, wrist, thigh
and the incoherent
hair, waterfalling
over the folds of her body
mollified
by the late sun.
Or it might have been
a wheatfield, light eddying
back and forth over
cool limbs, moulding
shoulder and breast from shadow.
It is a woman whom
breezes winnow and flail
on the hillside, alone,
a woman whom mobile light
slenderly tricks out
with arch of loin and belly,
it is a girl
beyond geology.

The fine grain of her skin
dissolves into landscape.

The Stones

In the wake of light the hills
shook and fell silent,

the rifts healing with lichen, small trees
disguising subsidence, while

the underground process,
as a moraine slow,

deliberate, hollowed the sheer
granite from within, caved out

uneasy quarters, a hiding-
place until the rivers,

done with their subterfuge,
could openly flow on.

But memories of ice
persist in their undertow,

these scoured valleyheads
where once the glacier started,

terrains of unusual quietness,
do not relax. Giant stones stand guard

against what day? Their granite
integrity,

heroic among farms,
even under the immense

burden of sun and water
will not give — not shelter,

not sustenance; at most
solidarity, with the light.

Where, after this false start,
how, do we turn back? how

begin afresh
with all our precious wisdom

scattered like discretion
to the winds and now

surely somewhere growing,
growing inarticulate
as stones.

March

The snow recedes,
the land breeds flies,
fresh leaf will adumbrate
the lawns of the old people's home,
a harsh sun
elicit answers, disinter skeletons
– drowned boats, rusted cars –
of marshlands, railway yards,
the whole decaying truth
that the snow's candour glossed.
Order will give way again
to growth.

Landmarks

It is possible
where now the excavators grub
to imagine a typist's face
at a tenth floor window
suspended
like a baroque cherub's.

It is possible
to think of the farmlands behind
built over, battened down,
away from sight and memory
or framed by glass and girders.

Who, though, can conceive
his own future absence, look into his own
dining-room and between his wife
and his small children imagine
an emptiness? Surely,
that too is possible.

My Death

I met my death today
as I walked across a bridge.
He's a swinger and dressed to kill
but his smile set my teeth on edge.

The face seemed familiar.
Where had we met before?
Once, ill with pneumonia,
I had crept past his door
and once when I nearly drowned
a few yards from the shore.
It seems he lives underground.

When I asked him in for a drink
he murmured with a frown
'I've my own cellar to attend to:
it's a good year for laying down.'

As I grow older he grows younger,
nourished on my decay.
But since nothing staunches his hunger
I have given up my anger,
entirely reconciled
to find on my porch some day
a screaming, abandoned child.

Stills

The face of a girl at a grilled window,
night landscapes from the train
haunting years afterwards
with possibilities;

snatches of peasant song, caught, lost again
on a mountain track towards sundown,
persisting as fragments;

not settled beauty, the orderly
schemings of palace gardens
or these at most only
under the weather, absorbing
change: beauty is anyway
a transient — millrace, birdflight, cloud,
the single, windfall gesture.

63061   PR
           6062
           E915
LEVENSON, CHRISTOPHER S7

STILLS.

DATE DUE